From Here to There

by Nancy Skultety • Illustrated by Tammie Lyon

Boyds Mills Press

Text copyright © 2005 by Nancy Skultety
Illustrations copyright © 2005 by Tammie Lyon
All rights reserved

Published by Boyds Mills Press, Inc.
A Highlights Company
815 Church Street
Honesdale, Pennsylvania 18431
Printed in China

Library of Congress Cataloging-in-Publication Data

Skultety, Nancy.
From here to there / by Nancy Skultety ; illustrated by Tammie Lyon.—1st ed.
p. cm.
Summary: A new road is built so Farmer Dibble can drive his truck to town.
ISBN 1-59078-092-2
[1. Road construction—Fiction.] I. Lyon, Tammie, ill. II. Title.

PZ7.S62865Fr 2004
[E]—dc22

2004014987

First edition, 2005
The text of this book is set in 16-point Stone Serif.
The illustrations are done in watercolor.

Visit our Web site at www.boydsmillspress.com

10 9 8 7 6 5 4 3 2

In loving memory of my parents, Earl Laney and Margaret Ann Klein Laney, who taught me the love of story.

With love to Terry, Breanne, Kolby, and Keely.

With gratitude to Kent Brown for believing in my work.

With love and special thanks to Terry and Angela for their expertise and to my friends and mentors Joy Cowley, Peter Catalanotto, and Jerry Spinelli.

—N. S.

For my mom, Diane Speer, whose unending pride and enthusiasm for everything I do has made this career possible and for my dad, Tom Speer, who thankfully passed on all those artistic genes!

—T. L.

Farmer Dibble drove to town. Bump! Bump! Bump!

"I want a road!" he cried.
"A road?" said the mayor.
"A road?" said the county
    engineer.
"A road from here to there,"
    said the surveyor.

Along came a flatbed truck with equipment.

It followed a pickup truck
with a crew to set up signs.

Push, push, push went the bulldozer.

Scoop, scoop, scoop went the front-end loader.

The dump trucks were filled with dirt.
They drove away, creaking and groaning.

Rumble, rumble! The grader smoothed the dirt.
Rumble, rumble! The compactor flattened the dirt.

The excavator dug
to lay drainpipes.
In went the pipes,
one by one.

The new road was ready for its blacktop coat.
It was time for the paver, time for the gravel truck.
Then along came the roller. Squish, Squish!

Swish, swish! The broom truck swept loose gravel off the road.
Wham, wham! In went the guardrails and road signs.

What else did the new road need?
A paint truck to paint the lines that mark the lanes!

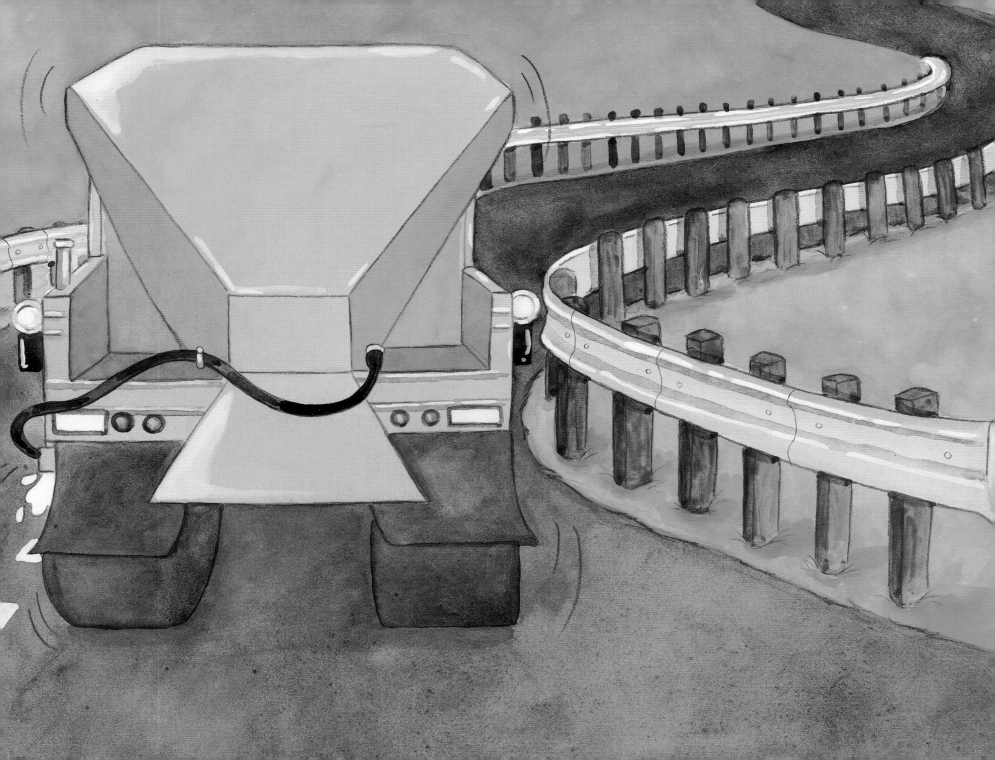

The crew had done a good job. Now they were finished.
The flatbed truck was loaded. The pickup truck, too.

"A new road
from here to there,"
said the surveyor.

All the people cheered.

Farmer Dibble drove to town.
"That's much better!" he cried.